**What people are saying about *BECOMINGS*. . .**

"Many of us speak of becoming one with nature, though few know how to proceed. *Becomings* provides a practical guide to experiencing kinship with nature. By following the suggestions offered, we experience our world from a new perspective. If we can come to understand our world through the eyes and lives of our co-inhabitants, we will be more willing to share our planet and treat it with the respect it deserves."

*John R. O'Meara, Director*
*Geauga Park District, Chardon, OH*

"As the demands of today's hurly burly world steadily increase, more and more people are seeking quiet and solitude. *Becomings*, a work born of that need to slow down, breathe deeply, and relax into the present moment, can act as an antidote to the frantic pace at which we drive ourselves."

*Anne A. Simpkinson, Editor*
Common Boundary

"Ellie Kings's *Becomings* reawakens the most precious parts of us—the innocent wisdom and wonder with which we entered this beautiful world. These imageries open delicious doorways to the joyous celebration of life's utter richness and sweetness."

*Cynthia Gale, Ceremonial Artist*

"It was a deep pleasure to experience these imageries. *Becomings* activates the natural child within. I believe this book would also appeal to children, helping to nurture their imaginations, and grounding their experiences of nature."

*John Parks, M.D., Director*
*Kentucky Center of Psychosynthesis*

# BECOMINGS

*A Unique Experience
of Our Earth*

# BECOMINGS

*A Unique Experience
of Our Earth*

## ELLIE KING

Illustrated by Mary Brigid

**Moonwillow
Press
Aurora, Ohio**

Moonwillow Press
P.O. Box 313, Aurora, Ohio 44202-0313, U.S.A.
Telephone: 440/543-8063

First Printing:
10 9 8 7 6 5 4 3 2 1


**Publisher's Cataloging in Publication**

King, Ellie. 1931-
    Becomings : a unique experience of our earth / by Ellie King. --
1st ed.
      p. cm.
      Includes bibliographical references.
      Preassigned LCCN: 97-73363
      ISBN: 0-9658594-5-2

    1. Visualization. 2. Imagery (Psychology) 3. Imagination. 4.
Nature--Meditations.   I.  Title.

BF367.K56 1997          158'.12
                     QB197-40773

Cover Design by Lavern Hall

 Printed on recycled, acid-free paper.

*To our beloved Earth*

*who has been so patient and forgiving*

*To all the becomings*

*written and unwritten*

*remembering*

*especially*

*those who become extinct*

*daily*

# CONTENTS

*Acknowledgments*                                      *x*
*Preface*                                              *xi*

Introduction                                           1
How To Use This Book                                   3
Opening Relaxation                                     5

The Becomings                                          7

  1.  An Inchworm                   9
  2.  A Rock                        13
  3.  Wind                          17
  4.  A Wolf                        21
  5.  Water                         25
  6.  A Fern                        29
  7.  Soil                          31
  8.  A Crow                        35
  9.  Fire                          41
10.  A Lion                                   45
11.  A Lioness                                49
12.  A Crocus                                 53
13.  A Dolphin                                55
14.  A Tree                                   59
15.  A Human Being                            63

*Suggested Readings*                                   67
  *Nature Books I Found of Interest*          69
  *Recommended Books on Visualization*        71
*About the Author*                                     73

## ACKNOWLEDGMENTS

My heart-felt thanks to all those who have given so graciously of their time and friendship during the writing of *Becomings*, encouraging me along the way.

For feedback and suggestions from Jean Benson, Joyce Dietrick, Susan Glassmeyer, Sharon Mandt, Dr. John Parks, Nancy Schneider, Sam Schneider, and Beth Streeter.

A special measure of gratitude to MaryAnn Myers for her many hours of wise counsel, and to Lavern Hall for sharing her knowledge with me, and guiding me through

And to Bob Paine, my dear husband and friend, always there to help me question, clarify, and refine.

# PREFACE

For as long as I can remember, I have felt close to nature. I have felt the aliveness of each unique entity, whether holding a stone in my hand and feeling its warmth or coolness; drinking in a magnificent skyfull of sunset; or quietly watching deer moving alertly through the forest with indescribable grace and elegance.

Some years ago, these imageries started nudging me. Eight of them emerged, and then I set them aside, involved with many other things in my life. Early last winter, they began nudging me again, only harder, seeming determined to be born into the world. Since then, they've been ever-present, calling me back if I'm too long away. This book you hold in your hands is the culmination of that birthing process.

# INTRODUCTION

When we were children, many of us had an every-day acquaintance with frogs, butterflies, and lightning bugs. Since then, with adult responsibilities and our busy daily lives, often we've drifted further and further from a close experience of earth and nature. And yet, in quiet moments, if we allow ourselves to sense and feel, we find a deep, quiet, inner longing for that lost, remembered closeness, whether beside the ocean, by a stream, or on a quiet walk through autumn leaves or soft spring air.

As children playing, we could become many things; whatever we imagined ourselves to be. This collection of becomings calls to that innate childhood ability. Each is an invitation to become, to explore, and to experience being; to reawaken and affirm our sense of knowing, wonder, and participation in oneness with the earth.

My hope is that you will experience, enjoy, and remember. . . And remember. . . And remember. . .

# HOW TO USE THIS BOOK

The becomings may simply be read and experienced and enjoyed.

They may be read to you by a friend, so you can relax totally into the experience of the visualization.

They may be used in a group setting, with sharing of experiences following the visualization.

Each becoming should be read slowly. . . . with ample time for experiencing. . . On the following page there is a simple relaxation which may be used at the beginning of each becoming.

As you travel through *Becomings*, you may find that you wish to bring some of your inner experiences and feelings into your outer world in more tangible form. Journaling, writing, drawing, painting, moving in ways your body wishes to move, dancing, allowing sounds to come, creating a song, working with clay, making or finding symbols for your experiences, taking action in the world on behalf of the becomings and the earth; all are ways of claiming, honoring, and grounding your experience.

## OPENING RELAXATION

Before experiencing each becoming, give yourself several moments of deep, unhurried breathing. . . . A time to slow down and disengage from your usual outside world . . . . . . . Breathing deeply and slowly. . . . Take a nice, full, cleansing breath. . . . Exhaling tension and worry. . . . And another full breath . . . . Breathing deeply and slowly . . . . . . . In and out . . . . At your own pace. . . . In your own way. . . . Nice, slow, deep breathing. . . . . . . Letting go. . . . Allowing tensions to soften. . . . To dissolve. . . . Slow, deep, peaceful breathing. . . . . . .

*A*nd now, when you are ready, become _____

# The Becomings

$\mathcal{A}$nd now, when you are ready. . . .

*Become an inchworm. . . . Experience your pale greenness. . . . Experience the bending flexibility of your body as you loop along, anchoring with your back legs, extending your body straight forward to grasp the branch. Then catching up with your back legs. . . . Looping along. Looping along. . . . Busy. Curious. Exploring the branch . . . . Taking each side road, twig after twig. Looping. Looping. Looping. . . . . . .*

*Suddenly a rush of wings, and a cardinal startles onto your branch. Danger! Too near! Danger! Down you drop on the silken thread spun from the gland beneath your jaw. Still. . . . Still. . . . Still. . . . . . . At last the cardinal, your enemy, flies across to another tree. . . .*

*As you dangle, a slight breeze gentles your body. . . . Enjoy the soft, swinging motion. . . . Sunlight shafting through the trees is warm and comforting. . . . . . .*

*Now you decide to gradually make your way back up to the branch . . . . Using your feet, you reel in your silken strand, zig-zagging your way steadily upward, toward a twig not much longer than you are. . . . Reaching the twig, you immediately anchor your back feet, and stiffly project your body out at an angle, perfectly mimicking and becoming part of the system of twigs . . . . Experience your body, totally rigid and still. . . . Imperceptible to bird enemies. . . . . . .*

*In time, you sense no imminent danger, and water droplets beckon on a nearby leaf. Relaxing your body from its survival rigidity, you bend in to re-engage the twig with your front feet. . . . The droplets call, and you loop toward them. . . . Now you pause to sense for danger. . . . Then loop into the welcome moisture. Experience rolling on your back in the droplets of water. . . . Feel the lovely, soothing wetness on your skin . . . . Experience the combined joys of movement, moisture, and well-being . . . . . . .*

*Now, become aware of your tiredness and need for rest . . . . Looping to the leaf's edge, you bite away small pieces, bit by bit making a hole just big enough to back into. . . . Now your camouflage along the leaf edge is complete. . . . And you can rest in the sun haze. . . . Enjoying the soft movement as your leaf host responds to intermittent passing breezes. . . . Contentment. . . . Peace. . . . . . .*

$\mathscr{A}$nd now, when you are ready. . . .

*Become a rock. . . . Feel the sunwarmth evenly on your sky surface. . . Feel the earthcoolness on your ground surface. . . Experience the sunwarmth and the earthcoolness mingling and blending inside of you. . . . . . .*

*Be aware of contact as a leaf's edges scrape across your sky surface, pushed by the wind. . . . A bird chooses to land upon you. Experience the interchange of pressures as it rests on you, preening in the sunwarmth. . . . Be aware of your solidness meeting its fragility. . . . . . Now, the bird's feet push against your solidness, its wings lifting quietly, as it continues on its journey, refreshed. . . . Your sky surface is again still. . . . Tree patterns of sun and shade make their way across your surface. . . . You find them comforting and peaceful. . . . . . .*

*Notice now the lengthening shadows. . . . The deepening of evening. . . . And the gradual coming of darkness. . . . . . . In the sun's absence, earthcoolness becomes nightcoolness. . . . Deep and moist. . . . Your stored sunwarmth wanes. . . . Moonlight glistens your sky surface. . . . Night creatures abound. There is occasional contact, as you meet with firm support, soft paws, or a scurrying insect. . . . . . .*

*You rest deeply. . . . Experiencing peace, and well-being with your place in the universe. . . . Your cool solidness contentedly awaits sunrise. . . . And the renewing of the cycle of sunwarmth and nightcoolness. . . . Set within the cycles of seasons. . . . Years. . . . Decades. . . . Centuries. . . . Millennia. . . . . . .*

*A*nd now, when you are ready. . . .

*Become wind. . . . Howling around corners and through tree branches. . . . Feel the rush and whoosh as you blow in gusts. . . . Experience your power. . . . Push against trees. Make them bend and sway. . . . Cause wheat fields to bend low to the ground, away from your intensity, wave after wave after wave. . . . Feel the power of forcing rain to an angle as it falls. . . . Experience sculpting snow into clean-lined drifts. . . . Enjoy squeezing through narrow places with concentrated force and speed, tumbling over yourself in your urgency and haste. . . . As you bombard the face of a cliff, feel your energy scatter magnificently. . . . . . . .*

*Now, deliciously spent, experience yourself in a playful mood. . . . Toy with a falling leaf. You send it spinning upward, breathless and surprised to have its descent interrupted and embroidered upon. . . . . . . Experiment with etching ripples and cat's-paws on a still lake, creating ever-changing patterns. . . . . . . Give gulls a force to lean into as they soar and bank. Enjoy the delicate interplay with their wings and bodies. . . . . . . Along mountain faces and peaks, abandon to the flow of your currents and sheers. . . . . . . Experience your swirls and eddies, stirring snowflakes in circles. . . .*

*Now, experience your gentleness, as you softly carry seeds, fragrances, and scents with you, giving messages for survival, and for pleasure. . . . . . . Experience the subtleties of being a warm spring breeze. . . . Welcomed, and breathed in deeply by animals, plants, and humans. . . . . . . . Sense the excitement, joy, and hope you bring as you pass by. . . . Experience blending your energy with grass . . . . A tree. . . . A stream. . . . Feel the sunlight exquisitely permeating your energy. . . . . . . Allow yourself to experience the unfolding sense of peace and oneness with the earth. . . . The sky. . . . The Universe. . . . . . .*

$\mathcal{A}$nd now, when you are ready. . . .

Become a wolf. . . . As you pause on a hilltop, experience your lean, compact, shaggy body. . . . Your warm fur. . . . Your strong muscular legs, which carry you in pursuit of food, and on your nomadic travels. . . . Test the early morning breeze with your acute sense of smell . . . . Your keen hearing. . . . Your sharp eyesight. . . . . . Your breath clouds in the chill air as you survey your surroundings. . . . Satisfied, you bend down and pick up the rabbit caught in your early morning hunting. You continue at an easy pace toward your den. . . .

As you reach your destination, you lay the rabbit on the ground. You gaze at your mate and your four sleeping pups . . . . You study each pup gently. . . . Each one distinct, already with its own ways. . . . You look at your young pack with love, and a feeling of responsibility. . . .

Your mate looks toward you. She rises, scanning the sleeping pups, and moves to where you are standing. . . . She crouches, gently biting you under the jaw, in greeting . . . . You softly take her long slim nose in your jaws, lightly closing them across the top of her nose. . . . Your tails wag with joy and comfort. . . . Together you eat a share of the meat. . . . This is your close companion for life, until one of you dies. When there were more in your pack, she was the dominant one of the females, as you were of the males. . . . The memory of the two-leggeds comes back. . . . *The loud, sharp noises.* . . . *Only you and your mate escaping . . . . . .*

*You look again toward your pups. They are yawning and stretching, and as they see each other, their tails wag in greeting. . . . Then, as they catch the scent of the morning feast, the hungry pups converge on your gift, pushing, growling, challenging for dominance. The gnawing hunger softens in their bellies. . . . . . .*

*When the meat is gone, their playful pouncing and tumbling begin immediately. . . . Your eyes soften as you watch them. They touch memories of before. . . . You are their protector, provider, and teacher. . . . Without your pack, it has been difficult while they are so young. No other wolves with whom to hunt large prey. No others to stay with the pups. You miss the comfort and assistance of the whole pack caring for and teaching the young ones. . . .*

*You watch the largest of the pups, measuring him as the emergent future leader. . . . Someday you will fall and not get up. He must be trained and strong, so your pack will survive. . . . . . .*

*You feel a contented happiness as you watch the pups. They are all healthy. They are growing and learning. A new pack is developing. . . . You are again taking your place among the other wolves. . . . You pull your lips back, revealing your white teeth, in an expression of pleasure. . . . You tilt your head back, and send up an undulating howl. . . . Your mate noses you affectionately. Her head tilts back, and her howl blends with yours. . . . The pups yip joyously, learning. . . . . . . . Off in the distance, there is an answering howl, joined by others. . . . . . . Yes, you are again taking your place among other wolf packs. You howl in answer, experiencing excitement. . . . Joy. . . . And peace. . . . At home in the Universe. . . . . . .*

$\mathcal{A}$nd now, when you are ready. . . .

Become water. . . . Experience your crystal clearness in
a woodland pond. . . . Transparent, yet reflecting. . . .
Placid. . . . Serene. . . . . . . Containing myriad forms
of life. . . . Be aware of their movements within you, even
as your clear surface gives back reflections to the sky, the
clouds, the trees. . . . Be aware of the greenness of your
mosses and plants. . . . Feel the interruption of your
surface by water bugs. . . . Their pleasant circles of ripples
gentling out into smoothness. . . .

Now experience your clearness bubbling over stones. .
. . Enjoy your soft voice as you encounter the stones,
choosing paths over and around. . . . Gently smoothing
their surfaces as you pass. . . . Gradually now, your pace
quickens, and the stones give way to bigger rocks, as the
stream bed makes its way down a hillside. . . . Experience
your excitement and playfulness as you encounter each rock,
sometimes swirling around its bulk, enjoying the graceful
patterns you create. . . . And sometimes matching surface
against surface, movement against stability, pitting force
against obstacle. Meeting in head-on confrontation.
Blatantly throwing your energy into the air in joyful
stubbornness and defiance. . . . . . .

At the bottom of the hill, you leave the rocks behind.
You now find yourself curving peacefully through
grasslands. . . . Notice the sounds of birds. . . .

*Animals come to your edges. You give to them gladly. . . . Experience the occasional eddies, as some of your energy is snagged into lazy circles near your banks. . . .*

*Now you experience a gradual quickening. A pull. . . . You feel yourself being swept into a wide, swift river. . . . Sense the excitement of purpose and direction, as you blend and become part of this greater force. . . . There is dignity and majesty in your movement now. . . . Anticipation. . . . There's an awareness of being swept along, not entirely of your own volition. . . . The river bed narrows, heightening your excitement and intensity. Your voice deepens into a constant, thunderous, roar. . . . You plunge ahead, totally committed to your course, experiencing a crescendo of velocity and power. . . . Suddenly, amidst the crescendo, in one shimmering moment, you break free, and find yourself H-U-R-T-L-I-N-G. . . . In slow motion. . . . Outward. . . . Into space. . . . Exhilarated and glistening. . . . Part of a graceful arc which curves toward the river below. . . .*

*Now, momentarily suspended in space, you become increasingly aware of the intensity of the sun. . . . The warmth pulls at you deeply, permeating your being. . . . Until almost without realizing that transformation is occurring, you surrender your form. . . . You float free in the diffuse form of soft mist. . . . Small wind currents lead you into swirls, reminiscent of your eddies as the river. . . . As you ascend higher and higher, you become aware of your sense of freedom. . . . And lightness. . . . And peace. . . . You are now able to look down on the turbulence of the waterfall below. As you float even higher and the* distance increases, you experience a deepening of the sense of freedom. . . . Lightness. . . . Peace. . . . . . .

Now become aware of the presence and the coming together of energies similar to your own. . . . Experience becoming one with these blending energies. . . . And gradually materializing in the form of a splendid cloud. . . . Enjoy your whiteness against the blue sky around you. . . . Explore your texture. . . . Form. . . . Movement. . . . Feel the sun constantly affecting your energy. . . .

Now you sense the atmosphere changing around you. Dark clouds have formed a barrier between you and the sun. . . . Cold grayness is everywhere. . . . . . . You experience the coldness pressing in on you, urging, compressing, insisting, until you again surrender your form, realizing you are losing your feeling of weightless freedom. Gravity pulls at you. . . . As you blend and combine with other droplets, a familiarity of form returns, and your excitement of purpose and direction is reawakened. . . . You re-connect with the magnitude of the returning water in the form of rain. . . . Experience being rain. . . . . . . Rain through wind and past trees. . . .

Experience splashing into a pond. Feel your impact on its surface. . . . Sending out ripples which bump other ripples in silent hills and valleys. . . . Experience your blending into oneness with the gentle waters. . . . Your ripples cease. . . . Experience becoming crystal clear. . . . Transparent, yet reflecting. . . . Experience giving back reflections to the sky, the clouds, the trees. . . . Experience yourself as placid. . . . Serene. . . . At peace. . . . . . .

*A*nd now, when you are ready. . . .

*Become a fern. . . . Feel green and cool. . . . Alive. Vibrant. Supple. . . . The air you are breathing is moist coolness. . . . Your whole environment is hushed, with soft mosses cushioning the sounds of birds and small creatures. . . . . . .*

*Experience your cool green fronds. . . . A small air current swirls by, and you nod and sway in response. Enjoy your delicate, graceful movements. . . . Become aware of your white, spidery roots spreading beneath the layer of mosses. . . . Your tubular stem, connecting roots and leaves. . . . Experience the exchange of nurturing fluids within. . . .*

*Feel the welcome, dappling of sunlight on your cool greenness, as tree leaves above respond to a high breeze. . . . Beneath your fronds, droplets of moisture pearl on the deep green mosses, and a toad blinks its eyes, thanking you for shelter. . . . A fly comes to rest on the sweet moss next to you, closely watched by your motionless guest. . . .*

*You contemplate the forest, pleasantly aware of each inhabitant, experiencing the peace and order of your world. . . . The sun again dapples your greenness, and a sense of gratitude wells up, settling into contentment at your place in the Universe. . . . . . .*

*A*nd now, when you are ready. . . .


Become soil. . . . Experience your dark, moist richness
. . . . Be aware of the many life forms within you, burrowing,
resting, seeking shelter. . . . Experience the roots of grasses,
plants, and trees. . . . Pushing, pushing, seeking moisture
and nutrients. . . . Experience anchoring the roots of a
tall tree pulled by strong wind. . . . . . .

Now experience yourself on a cliffside, mixed with shale,
existing symbiotically with tree roots. . . . Bits of your
vertical surface let go, cascading downward breathlessly,
in slow motion. . . . . . . Brave yellow dandelions make
their stand on your slope, surrounded by mosses trying to
make everything secure. . . . . . .

Now experience your texture as fine, sparkling sand,
deposited along the bank by a spring-swollen stream. . . .
Experience your fine creamy lightness in the sunwarmth. .
. . And your moist beigeness in rockshade. . . . Feel the
weight of rocks and sticks. . . . Sense a young wolf padding
across your surface to drink from the stream. . . . And
enjoy as she rolls on her back, tossing bits of your warm
surface, leaving the imprint of her presence when she is
gone. . . . . . .

Now experience yourself as clay. . . . Experience your
dense, cool, unyielding thickness. . . . Roots struggle to make
their way into your depths. . . . Delight in being so solid.
Impervious. Impenetrable. . . . . . .

*Now experience yourself as soft, murky ooze beneath a swamp. . . . Everything is brown. . . . Darkness, and almost darkness. . . . As you blur your being with the thick, still water, muted shafts of sunlight almost reach you . . . . Roots are welcome solidness as they take hold and deepen into your softness. They lend stimulation and stability. . . . . . .*

*Now experience yourself as ocean floor. . . . Wide. . . . Calm. . . . Majestic. . . . Experience your dark, secret expanse. Your wide, mysterious plains. . . . The grandeur of your mountains. . . . Your open volcanic fissures. . . . Meet the ocean's pressure with your solidness. . . . Experience the interplay of energy along your surface. . . . . . .*

*Now allow your awareness to widen and expand, joining with all of earth's surface. . . . Becoming the whole surface of planet earth. . . . . . . Retaining awareness of your varied textures. . . . Your formations. . . . Your altitudes . . . . Your depths. . . . Becoming the whole circumference of planet earth. . . . . . . Experience interacting with sunlight. . . . With water. . . . And with air. . . . Experience your revolving as you circle the sun. . . . Be aware of the presence of other planets in your Universe, and your relationship to them. . . . Experience your wholeness. . . . Your beauty. . . . . . .*

*A*nd now, when you are ready. . . .

*Become a crow. . . . Experience your body. . . .*
*Black, with shimmerings of deep blue & purple. . . . Look*
*around from your roosting place high in a pine tree. . . .*
*You can see for a long distance. . . . On one side, the*
*woods offer roosting trees and shelter for assembling. . . .*
*On the other, farm lands open wide, with special*
*opportunities for food. . . . And beyond, the noisy highways*
*of constant movement, where animals often die. . . .*

*It's dawning. You stretch your wings, and become aware*
*of your hunger. . . . You take off from your roost, with a*
*relaxed CAW CAW CAW, inviting others to join you in*
*your morning search for food. Experience your wings as*
*they move slowly and deliberately in flight, with regular,*
*even wingbeats against the supporting air. . . . Feel the*
*air parting as you move through. . . . Others of your*
*friends are flying too, in a loosely-formed flock. You fly*
*toward the corn fields. This is the time of seedsprouting. . . .*
*No two-leggeds in sight. Only the still sticks dressed like a*
*two-legged. You scornfully land on its hat, waiting for the*
*others to gather. . . . Now you all settle on the field,*
*savoring the tender sprouts. . . . A sharp crack reverberates.*
*A two-legged with a killing stick! CAW! CAW! CAW! CAW!*
*Great danger! The dispersal call is given, and the flock*
*scatters instantly. Your wings beat hard and evenly, carrying*
*you away from the field. . . .*

*As you fly, you hear the call of a friend, and you both turn toward the highway. . . . You settle together onto the dirt near the road. No newly-killed animals in sight here, but you feel the vibrations with your feet as the big, many-wheeled, noisy ones pass by. You exchange glances, and wait. . . . The ground surface near you stirs, and an earthworm emerges, brought to the surface by the vibrations. You and your friend feed, and wait. . . . Feed, and wait. Grateful for food. . . . When your hunger is appeased, you spread your wings, again committing yourself to the supportive air. Drawing your legs up under your body, you rise above the incessant and oppressive din, and again enjoy the loveliness of flying. . . . The subtle control of direction . . . . The sunlight on your wings. . . . You are aware of others from your flock, hearing their individual calls as they forage for food. . . .*

*Your friend whizzes by, playfully inviting you to chase. You accept, increasing the force of your wings against the air, climbing, turning, diving, trying to anticipate your friend's moves. Calling out in challenge and enjoyment. . . . Finally, energy spent, you both settle onto branches in adjacent trees, cawing to each other. . . . Resting. . . . In the meadow below, cows are drowsing. You decide to play some more. Launching from your branch, you swoop down over the unsuspecting cows, and tweak at the nearest ear. . . . Returning to your branch, you caw your mischievous joy. Your friend caws his approval, then leaves his roost, and duplicates your performance. Together, you caw raucously at the hapless cows. . . .*

*Suddenly, you hear the assembly call! Predator! Predator! Instantly you fly toward the call. A hawk has been detected in the flock's territory, and is being mobbed, amidst clammoring cawing. You join in, as your family and friends, in great and persistent numbers, fly at the hawk, loudly threatening and harassing, making clear their territory and their intention that he leave. . . . The hawk, relinquishing, and deciding to try again another day, flies away from your roosting woods. . . . Across the fields. . . . . . .*

*You and the flock settle on your roosting places, victorious and self-satisfied. . . . There is some bickering, here and there, over a favored roost, accompanied by threat calls. . . . The young crows take this time for play. . . .*

*You decide to take one last flight in the fast-changing light of the setting sun. Your wingspan is wide and sure. . . . As you survey the ground beneath you, an object glints in the slanting rays of the sun. You fly lower to investigate. . . . Your inquisitiveness brings you to rest beside a round, sparkling object connected to a long, bright chain. You pick it up in your beak, and push off into the air. The chain comes loose and drops away, and you carry your glittering prize across to the edge of the meadow, to the base of a small fir tree. You look around to see if you are being observed. . . . It seems safe. You set your treasure down, pushing and turning it with your beak. It is beautiful! The sun is below the horizon, so you carefully bury your shiny new find beneath the small tree. . . . . . .*

*Your wings lift you smoothly in flight, and you enjoy the evening coolness as you soar and descend. . . . Now you return to the sheltering woods, and amidst your flock, find a comfortable roosting place for the night. . . . Your friend nearby sends you a soft, acknowledging CAW. . . . Your heart holds happiness at your place in the Universe. . . . You are tired. . . . And content. . . . You look forward to returning in the daylight to your new-found discovery. . . . Your tiredness and contentedness blend, and you settle on your roost into a peaceful, quiet rest. . . . . . .*

$\mathcal{A}$nd now, when you are ready. . . .

*Become fire. . . . Experience your hot brilliance. Your
orangeness. . . . Feel your darting movements, as you lick
around a log, searching for crevices and niches where
you can take hold. . . . The deep red coals are solid and
nurturing beneath your busy, exploring flames. . . . The
intense heat sustains your sporadic, whirring, blue updrafts,
and your contented yellow dancings. . . . Experience
systematically consuming each stick and log, as you
methodically transform the wood into a glowing, pulsing
core, covered with gray ash. . . . Radiant heat. . . . Thin,
white smoke. . . . Enjoy your voice through the process. . . .
Crackling. Spitting. Popping. Roaring. . . . . . .*

*Experience yourself tamed and domesticated within a
fireplace or open campfire. . . . Cultivated, and welcome.
Fed paper, kindling, and logs to consume. Urged and coaxed
into being. Within limits. Controlled. Enjoy the contented,
easy sharing of your warmth and companionship with
humans and animals. . . . Radiate your warmth to faces,
hands, and bodies; changing the air around them for
pleasure, and for survival. . . . . . .*

*Now experience yourself coming to life in a forest. . . .
Experience your quiet, early smoldering. . . . Your tentative,
thin flaming. . . . Sense your gradual awareness that there
is no one to control you. To limit you. . . . . Experience
hungrily consuming ground cover, gaining confidence that*

*no one can contain you. . . . Welcome the wind's help in widening your path. . . . Feel your excitement grow as you realize your power. . . . Underbrush flames. Trees blaze. Animals flee. You are everywhere. Your unleashed raw energy roars, "I am! I am! I am!". . . . . . .*

*When finally you reach the forest's edge, your energy ebbing, you become a quiet, spent smoldering. . . . Your smoke is everywhere. . . . Your helper, the wind, has become more gentle, and softly nudges the smoke into patterns of dispersal. . . . In the quietness, you are aware of a sense of oneness. . . . The forest floor will now rest and prepare itself for new life and growth. . . . Gratitude glows within you for your place in the Universe. . . . You are tired and content. . . . . . .*

*A*nd now, when you are ready. . . .

*Become a lion. . . . Experience your body. . . . Your magnificent head on its strong thick neck. . . . Your mane, freshly-groomed, and intimidating. . . . Your firm, muscular body. . . . Your legs, with big paws firmly planted. . . . Now experience your long tail, with its thick end tuft. Enjoy directing the movements of your tail. . . . . . .*

*The other male lion with you is your close friend and companion. Together, you are patrolling and marking the boundaries of your territory. Defending ownership of your two prides of females, who provide you with food and cubs. . . . Experience roaring. . . . From low growls and groans to full-volumed, thunderous, bellowing roars. . . . Feel your power all through your body. . . . Affirm your sureness and mastery as you roar. . . . Communicating your presence. . . . Declaring your territory. . . . . . .*

*Now, you begin to move forward. . . . Silently. . . . Effortlessly. . . . Experience the smooth interaction of your muscles. . . . Enjoy the gracefulness with which you move. . . . . . . Now you decide to run, for the sheer joy of wind, and swift, perfect movement. . . . Your companion joins you. Experience your body. . . . Be aware of all parts of your being working rhythmically together at your bidding . . . . Experience your ease and exhilaration. . . . . . .*

*Now, gradually slow your pace, looking out through your eyes at your world. . . . Be aware of your impact on other creatures. . . . You check the breeze for scents, sounds, movement, always alert to danger or opportunity. . . . Satisfied, you and your friend roll and stretch luxuriously in the tall grasses, rubbing your heads and backs against the earth. . . . Absorbing the soft deep warmth of the sunlight on your fur. . . . Experience the joy of being alive . . . . . . .*

In the near distance, three vultures circle in the sky above your territory. . . . All your senses alert, you set off together, toward possible food. . . . As you near the center of the circling, you come upon three of the females from one of your prides, consuming their fallen prey, a gazelle. You and your friend charge in. The females scatter, each one growling, and taking a share of the meat with her. Together, you and your companion eat, assuaging your hunger. . . . . . .

Leaving the carcass to the waiting hyenas, you set off toward the pride. . . . As you approach, you hear cubs tussling in the grass beyond the rocks. . . . The boldest cubs welcome your arrival, two of them bounding expectantly toward you. And one crouching in ambush, watching intently. The others are nursing, or stretched out absorbing the warm sunlight. You nuzzle the cubs who approach you, breathing in their familiar scent. . . . They rub against your face and legs. . . . The third cub finally pounces, and joins in the nuzzling and rubbing. . . .

You climb to the top of the rocks, checking the breeze for scents, and then choose a comfortable place to lie down. . . . Contentedly, you watch the females and cubs *below. . . . Soon, one of the females climbs up the rocks and lies down beside you. . . . She touches you softly with her paw, and drapes her tail across your back. . . . You lick her face and head gently with your rough tongue. . . . The same three cubs tumble over and around you, attacking your mane. . . . And pouncing on your tail tuft. . . . The sun is soft and warm. . . . The breeze gentle and safe. . . . Your eyes close part-way. . . . Peace and well-being fill you. . . . . . .*

*A*nd now, when you are ready. . . .

*Become a lioness. . . . Experience your body. . . . Your smooth, fluid movements. . . . Your solidness. . . . Your controlled power. . . . Experience stretching. . . . Curling your tail over your back, and tensing your strong muscles . . . . Your alert senses check the breeze. . . . Your sisters have gone to hunt food, and this time you stayed with the cubs. They are all sleeping, some in the sunwarmth, and some in the rockshade. . . .*

*Your energy is restless. . . . You can hear the males roaring as they patrol the boundaries of their territory, defending their ownership of your pride. . . . Purposefully, you stride toward a nearby tree. With your forepaws, you reach up the trunk, languorously sharpening your extended claws on the rough brown bark. . . . Enjoy the stretch of your muscles. . . . . . .*

*You again check the scents on the breeze as you turn back toward the cubs. . . . You stretch out, watching and guarding. Several of the cubs begin to stir, yawning and stretching, blinking in the sunlight. . . . They tumble toward you, and you accept the searching, pushing little mouths as they nurse. . . . One of them is your own cub. The others from your sisters. . . . Experience licking the furry little faces, heads, and bodies with your raspy tongue. Enjoy their scent. The little faces and bodies rub against you, in love and dependence. . . . . . .*

*In the near distance, three vultures circle in the sky over your hunting territory. Your sisters have found food, and will soon be back with you. . . . It is good to be in the companionship and comparative safety of the pride. Life as a solitary nomad is difficult, filled with danger, and very lonely. . . . Experience the tightening in your abdomen in anticipation of food from the hunt. You rise to a sitting position, your senses alert. . . .*

*Your favorite sister, who is still without cubs, returns first, carrying meat in her jaws. She rushes at you playfully, knocking you over with her shoulder. You swat at her affectionately with soft paws, and she drops her gift in front of you. You eat hungrily, experiencing the tightness in your abdomen subside. . . . As your other sisters return, the awakened cubs tumble toward them, and each accepts the searching, pushing little mouths as they nurse. The cubs are nuzzled and licked. . . .*

*Now, stretch out in the soft sunlight. . . . Happiness fills you. . . . Your sister drapes her tail across your flank, and licks your face and head. . . . Lying there among the close circle of your sisters and your cubs, you feel a close companionship. . . . Contentment. . . . Peace. . . . . . .*

*A*nd now, when you are ready. . . .

*Become a crocus. . . . It is the underground time of resting. . . . Of being. . . . Experience the ground warm around you, blanketed and snug under the snow. . . . It is not yet the time of becoming. . . . It is the time of waiting . . . . Experience your concentrated, dormant energy. . . . Your impatience for spring is a vague longing. . . . . . .*

*Time passes. . . . Your fullness becomes ready. Complete. . . . Your impatience for spring and becoming grows more and more intense. . . . Waters are trickling down around you, signaling melting snows. . . . Warm energy of sunlight on the ground's surface calls to your fullness. Your longing. . . . You feel yourself responding. Opening. . . . An almost claustrophobic pushing begins. Upward, upward. Toward the ground's surface. Unwilling to wait to be sure. . . . You must find out for yourself. . . .*

*Your shoots break through the ground. . . . Push through the layer of white. . . . And up into sunlight. . . . You emerge above ground and snow, realizing you are purple with green leaves. . . . You are excited. Alive. . . . And you can breathe deeply. . . . You feel the sun's thin, early springwarmth, and you know you did what you had to do. . . . Your bravery stands etched in purple and green amidst the snow. . . . . . .*

*A*nd now, when you are ready. . . .


*Become a dolphin.  . . . Experience your sleek body gliding smoothly through the deep water. . . . Undulating. Up and down.  . . . Enjoy the sensations of the water against your skin.  . . . Now, swimming upward, you bring your blowhole above the surface, taking a breath of air without interrupting the smooth rhythm of your forward motion. . . . And again submerging beneath the surface. . . .*

*You swim with your family, which is part of a still larger group of dolphins. You see your mother nearby with her newly-born calf swimming at her side. You watch as the baby nurses on the milk squirted into his mouth from his mother. You feel protectiveness and love for the new little one. . . .*

*Now, your favorite friend noses you playfully. She dives, inviting you to chase. As she surfaces again, she tosses a piece of seaweed to you. Catching it easily, you take it with you, circling, diving, teasing as she pursues. . . . Experience the water, the sunlight, the feeling of your muscles working in synchrony as you play. . . . Now you rise to take a breath. . . . And as she breaks surface, you toss the seaweed back to her. . . .*

*You both stop. There is a signal. An alert spreads through your family pod. A large school of fish is near. Quietly, you join your family, skillfully encircling the school of fish, herding them into a smaller and smaller area. . . . When it is your turn, you charge through the school to feed. . . .*

*Now, in the distance you hear the motor noise of one of the human floatings coming toward you. . . . Together, you and your friend swim toward the noise to investigate. . . . As you draw closer, the humans on the floating turn toward you, putting black circle eyes up in front of their faces. They point at you with their strange flippers, and more of them appear. . . . Some make sounds and wave. Some stand quietly, looking through their black circles. . . . You feel curiosity and kinship with these strange creatures. You wonder about them and where they come from. . . . You remember coming upon one alone in the water about two moons ago. You'd circled it, and then approached. It had made sounds to you. . . . You'd stayed with it, circling for a long time, until a noisy, shiny bird with whirling wings and another human in its belly had swooped down and picked it up. It had waved to you and called out as the bird took it away. . . . The water had seemed quiet after it was gone. . . . You wonder about these creatures, and where they come from, and where they go. . . . You wonder if that one from the water is on the floating. . . . . .*

*Playfully you signal your friend. You both dive deep into the water, turning together and swimming powerfully toward the surface. . . . Together you breach in perfect synchrony, much to the excitement of the humans on the floating. They make many sounds, some hitting their flippers together, and some still looking through their little black circles. . . . You enjoy their attention. . . . Their energy joins with yours. . . . A sense of well-being spreads through you. . . . Experience diving. . . . Breaching. . . . Circling the floating. . . . Enjoy the warmth of the sunlight. . . . The sensations of the cold water. . . . The sounds of the humans . . . . Experience the energy of their enjoyment, curiosity, and feelings of affection intermingling with yours. . . . You wonder again if that one from the water is on this floating. . . . . . .*

*A*nd now, when you are ready. . . .

Become a tree. . . . a tall, beautiful tree. . . . Take the time you need to discover what kind of tree you are. . . . Experience yourself as a tree. . . . Sense your trunk. . . . Your roots. . . . Your branches. . . . . . .

Now, let all your attention go to your roots. Experience being roots. . . . Searching for moisture. Extending. Deepening. . . . Experience the soil you are pushing through. Its consistency. Its temperature. . . . Experience your strength. . . . Your width and depth. . . . Your holding power. . . . Anchoring the tree. . . . . . .

Now, let all your attention go to your trunk. Experience being the trunk. . . . Experience your solidness and stability . . . . Sense your bark. Its texture. Its color. . . . Experience your shape and thickness. . . . Your flexible response to wind and the pull of branches above. . . . Experience your strength and resilience. . . . You are the connection between roots and branches. You carry the life force. . . . . . .

Now, let all your attention go to your branches. Experience being branches. . . . Feel your movement. Your freedom. Your swaying. . . . Dance in wind. . . . Reach toward sky. . . . Feel sunlight on your leaves. . . . Notice and enjoy birds and animals which you shelter. . . . Perhaps there are children who escape for solitude into your peaceful holding. . . . Your leaves nurture the tree, and make it possible for humans and animals to survive. Enjoy your stillness. . . . And your swaying. . . . . . .

*Now, let your attention widen again to experience yourself as the whole tree. . . . . . . . Be aware of your wide, deep, anchoring roots. . . . Your strong, resilient trunk. . . . Your free, sheltering branches and life-giving leaves. . . . Take the time you need to fully experience your wholeness. Your completeness. . . . . . . Reach deep into the earth. . . . Reach high toward the sky. . . . Sense the connecting flow of energy and fluids through your trunk. . . . You welcome sunlight. . . . Wind. . . . Stillness . . . . Rain. . . . Snow. . . . You are glad for your place between earth and sky. . . . Experience your integrity. . . . Your knowing. . . . Your peace. . . . . . .*

*A*nd now, when you are ready. . . .

*Again become a human being. . . . Gently bring your awareness back into your own body. . . . Take a moment to re-experience yourself as a human being. . . . Feel the earth beneath your feet. . . . The air surrounding you. . . . Experience your breathing. . . . . . .*

*And now, holding in your heart all your experiences of becoming, find before you an inviting path. You decide to see where it leads. . . . The air is soft and warm, tree leaves sparkle, and the variety of birds' songs amazes you. . . .*

*You continue walking along the path, and soon find yourself in a lovely meadow. . . . You pause, drinking in the visual beauty. . . . The warmth of the sun. . . . The gentle breeze. . . . The fragrances. . . . The sounds. . . . The textures. . . . . . .*

*The path beckons you on toward a soft, sun-dappled forest at the meadow's edge. . . . As you enter the shade of the trees, your skin delights in the cool moistness. . . . You feel a grateful peace as you continue your journey. . . . You are aware that your presence in the forest is known by many creatures. . . . . . .*

*As you walk, you notice the path begins a gentle climb, choosing its way up a hillside. . . . Pine trees keep you company as you climb. . . . You feel the sun's warmth on your shoulders after the forest coolness. . . . You continue upward on the path, and soon you can look out over the trees below. . . . Your climb now leads you up a steeper slope. . . . The sun has become hot, and presses down on your head and shoulders. . . . Your throat is dry. . . . Just as you feel you can climb no further, you crest the steep rise. Gratefully, you accept the shade offered by a tall, old tree. . . . Settling back against the trunk, you rest, gazing out across a beautiful valley, experiencing the loveliness and peace. . . . A breeze cools your forehead. Your eyes take in the incredible view. . . . The contrasts. . . . Light and shadow. . . . Textures. . . . Colors. . . . Movement . . . . Stillness. . . . . . .*

*A deep, profound love of the earth and her creatures wells up within you. . . . Yet haunted and shadowed by sadness and helpless despair at the pollution and destruction caused by your own species: human beings. . . .*

*You remember all your experiences of becoming. . . . Each animal, plant, bird, and element is within you, is a part of you. . . . As you remember, and go deep inside yourself, there may be one of your becomings to whom you are especially drawn. . . . . . . Sense its presence. . . . Experience being together. . . . . . Experience how this becoming is being affected by human beings. . . . . . . What does it want to tell you? What does it want you to know. . . . . . . Listen to what it has to teach you. . . . Share the feelings in your heart. . . . . . . Ask any questions you may have, and listen to the answers. . . . . . . . Experience and receive the special wisdom it has for you. . . . . . .*

*Now, as you look out across this beautiful valley, you think about your becomings and what you've experienced . . . . How can you help the earth and her creatures? What can you do? What can you do yourself? . . . . . . Consciously decide on one way you will help our planet; one thing you can do in your own life to help the earth. Take the time you need to choose what you will do. . . . . . .*

*Now, imagine yourself doing what you've chosen. . . . . . . Visualize it. . . . . . . Experience it all through your body. . . . . . Deepen your promise to the earth. . . . . . . And to your becomings. . . . . . .*

*And now, get up, leaving your despair behind, and return to the path, finding your way down the hillside. . . . . . . Walk back through the coolness of the forest. . . . Then the brightness of the meadow. . . . And back to where you first joined the path. . . . . . .*

*Your becomings are forever a part of you. . . . Remember your chosen way to help the earth. . . . . . And do it. . . . . . .*

# Suggested Readings

# NATURE BOOKS I FOUND OF INTEREST

Allen, Durward L., & Mech, L. David. "Wolves Versus Moose on Isle Royale." *National Geographic*: Vol. 123, No. 2. Feb, 1963.

Anderson, Harald T. *The Biology of Marine Mammals.* New York: Academic Press, 1969.

Busch, Robert. *The Wolf Almanac.* New York: Lyons & Burford, 1995.

Caldwell, David K., & Caldwell, Melba C. "Senses and Communication." In *Mammals of the Sea: Biology and Medicine*, Sam Ridgeway, (Ed.). Springfield, IL: Charles C. Thomas, 1972.

Chapman, Joseph A. *Wild Mammals of North America: Biology, Management, And Economics.* Baltimore: Johns Hopkins Unversity Press, 1982.

Hanby, Jeannette. *Lions Share: The Story of a Serengeti Pride.* Boston: Houghton Mifflin, 1982.

Harrison, Richard & Bryden, M.M. *Wales, Dolphins and Porpoises.* New York: Facts on File Publications, 1988.

Haas, Emmy. *Pride's Progress: The Story of a Family of Lions.* New York: Harper & Row, 1967.

Leatherwood, Stephen, & Reeves, Randall R. *The Sierra Club Handbook of Whales and Dolphins.* San Francisco: Sierra Club Books, 1983.

Lopez, Barry Holstun. *Of Wolves and Men.*, New York: Scribner, 1978.

Martin, Dr. Anthony R. *The Illustrated Encyclopedia of Whales and Dolphins.* New York: Portland House, 1990.

Mech, L. David. *The Arctic Wolf: Living with the Pack.* Stillwater, MN: Voyageur Press, 1988.

Mech, L. David. *The Way of the Wolf.* Stillwater, MN: Voyageur Press, 1991.

Mech, L. David. "Where Can the Wolf Survive?" *National Geographic:* Vol. 152, No. 2. Oct, 1977.

Montgomery, Steven L. "The Case of the Killer Caterpillars." *National Geographic*: Vol. 164, No. 2. Aug, 1983.

Norris, Kenneth S. *The Porpoise Watcher*. New York: W.W. Norton and Company, 1974.

Pringle, Laurence P. *Listen to the Crows.* New York: Crowell, 1976.

Savage, Candace Sherk. *Wolves*. San Francisco: Sierra Club Books, 1988.

Swain, Ralph Brownlee. *The Insect Guide: Orders and Major Families of North American Insects.* Garden City, New York: Doubleday, 1948.

Watson, Lyall. *Sea Guide to Whales of the World.* New York: Dutton, 1981.

Wilmore, Sylvia Bruce. *Crows, Jays, Ravens, and their Relatives.* Middlebury, VT: Paul S. Erikson, 1977.

# RECOMMENDED BOOKS ON VISUALIZATION

Adair, Margo. *Working Inside Out: Tools For Change.* Applied Meditation For Intuitive Problem Solving. Berkeley, CA: Wingbow Press, 1984.

Andersen, Marianne S., and Savary, Louis M. *Passages: A Guide For Pilgrims of the Mind.* New York: Harper & Row, 1972.

Bry, Adelaide, and Bair, Marjorie. *Directing the Movies of Your Mind: Visualization For Health And Insight.* New York: Harper & Row, 1978.

de Mille, Richard. *Put Your Mother On the Ceiling: Children's Imagination Games.* New York: Penguin, 1976.

Drury, Nevill. *Inner Health: The Benefits of Relaxation, Meditation, & Visualization.* San Leandro, CA: Prism Press, 1985.

Epstein, Gerald. *Healing Visualizations: Creating Health Through Imagery.* New York: Bantam Books, 1989.

Ferrucci, Piero. *What We May Be.* Los Angeles: J.P.Tarcher, Inc., 1982.

Fugitt, Eva D. *He Hit Me Back First: Creative Visualization Activities for Parenting and Teaching.* Rolling Hills Estates, CA: Jalmar Press, 1983.

Gawain, Shakti. *Creative Visualization.* New York: Bantam Books, 1982.

Gendlin, Eugene. *Focusing.* New York: Bantam Books, 1979.

Levine, Stephen. *Healing Into Life and Death.* New York: Doubleday, 1987.

Mason, L. John. *Guide to Stress Reduction.* Berkeley, CA: Celestial Arts, 1985.

Naparstek, Belleruth. *Staying Well with Guided Imagery.* New York: Warner Books, 1994.

Naparstek, Belleruth. *Health Journeys.* (Audio Cassette Series). Cleveland, OH: Image Paths, 1991-1997.

Samuels, Mike. *Seeing With the Mind's Eye: The History, Techniques, And Uses Of Visualization.* New York: Random House, 1975.

Simonton, O. Carl, Matthews-Simonton, Stephanie, and Creighton, James L. *Getting Well Again.* Los Angeles: J. P. Tarcher, Inc., 1978.

## ABOUT THE AUTHOR

Ellie King, LISW, holds a Bachelor's Degree in Psychology from Kent State University, and a Master's Degree in Social Work from Case Western Reserve University. She also completed the 3-year training at the Kentucky Center of Psychosynthesis, and has utilized imagery in her practice of psychotherapy across many years. She has led numerous workshops, worked with hospice, presented Womangathering retreats, taught visualization, and served as consultant to other therapists in their use of imagery with clients. In *Becomings*, she has taken great joy in combining the art of guided imagery with her beloved world of nature. She lives with her husband in Bainbridge Township, Ohio.

## ORDER FORM

Name _____

Address _____

City_____ State_____ Zip _____

Telephone (     )_____

Please send _____ copies of *Becomings: A Unique Experience of Our Earth* @ $9.95 per copy.

**Shipping:** Add $2.00 for the first book, and 50¢ for each additional book. In Ohio, please include 57¢ sales tax per book.

I am enclosing $_____(check or money order) payable to Moonwillow Press.

**Send orders to:**

Moonwillow Press
P.O. Box 313
Aurora, OH 44202-0313  U.S.A.

**Inquiries:** (440)543-8063